ARTISTS ON BALI

ARTISTS ON BALI

W. O. J. Nieuwenkamp

Rudolf Bonnet

Walter Spies

Willem Hofker

A. J. Le Mayeur

Arie Smit

Ruud Spruit

THE PEPIN PRESS

AMSTERDAM · KUALA LUMPUR

First published by The Pepin Press BV in 1995

ISBN (HARDCOVER EDITION)   90 5496 025 6
ISBN (SOFTCOVER EDITION)   90 5496 018 3

A CIP record for this book is available from the publisher
and from the Royal Dutch Library, The Hague.

Designed and produced by
The Pepin Press
POB 10349
1001 EH Amsterdam
The Netherlands
Fax 31 20 4201152

Translated by Dr Robert Lankamp

Printed and bound in Singapore

Front cover: BONNET, *Portrait of a man*,
1933, pastel.
Back cover: HOFKER, *Ni Dablig weaving*,
1939, pastel.
Right: BONNET, *Portrait of a lady*,
undated, pastel.
Page 6: SMIT, *Galungan Ceremony*,
1991, acrylic on canvas.

CONTENTS

INTRODUCTION

The Dutch on Bali

In 1595 four ships under Cornelis de Houtman and Pieter Dirkszoon Keyser undertook the first Dutch exploration for spices in Asia. Experience in fishing the dangerous waters off Holland had provided the Dutch with sufficient seamanship and expertise in naval construction.

In the course of the sixteenth century there was an increase in Dutch trade with Baltic and Mediterranean countries. Transshipment turned out to be the most profitable form of trade. Timber, furs and wheat were brought from Scandinavia and the Baltic to the Mediterranean. From the South, salt and wine were transported north. Contacts with traders in Venice, Genoa, Spain and Portugal led to trade in exotic prod-

ucts such as porcelain, silk, carpets, majolica, and especially the urgently coveted spices pepper, cloves and nutmeg. The spice trade was the most profitable enterprise, especially when it proved possible to eliminate the middlemen by acquiring the spices at the source. Dutch merchants dreamt of the large profits that could be made once the route to the spice lands had been discovered. The Dutch grabbed their chance when the situation in Europe changed dramatically. The sixteenth century brought various changes: floods tormented the land, epidemics took their toll of countless victims, crops repeatedly failed, the economy declined, the political situation was unstable and resistance against the hegemony of the Roman Catholic church had led to reform movements.

Charles V, whose empire encompassed a large portion of Europe, including the Netherlands, was able to forcefully contain the unrest. But under his successor, the fanatical and devout Philip II, the empire fell apart. Led by Prince William of Orange, the Dutch rebelled. Philip II made the grave error of expelling the Jews —

Left: *Poster by Willem Hofker for the Bali Hotel*, probably printed in 1938 or 1939.

who included many merchants with contacts in Asia — from Spain and Portugal. Also, he intended to subjugate the Netherlands with a great show of force. This led to a guerilla war lasting eighty years in the wet Netherlands. The southern Netherlands — present-day Belgium — were defeated, which meant the end of prosperity for the mercantile city of Antwerp. In the northern Netherlands the enemy repeatedly routed. The result was that Antwerp merchants and Jewish businessmen from Spain and Portugal, with their capital and their contacts, settled in the northern Netherlands, the present-day Netherlands. Their goal was to break the Spanish and Portuguese trade monopoly with Asia and the Americas.

In Holland, intensive studies were done of charts, logs and journals which had been secretly compiled by sailors in the service of Spain. Around 1590, they concluded that it was feasible to reach the spice islands, either by sailing around Africa and the Cape of Good Hope, or by finding a passage through the Arctic. The voyage to the Arctic was a complete failure because the ships got stuck in the ice. But the Dutch ships that followed the southern route in 1595 succeeded in reaching Java and Bali.

The First Dutch Voyage to Java and Bali

The first voyage to Asia was organized by a strange company consisting of Antwerp refugees, German Baptists and Dutch Calvinists. They made use of the experience of men such as Jan Huygen van Linschoten, who while in Portuguese service made a voyage to Goa, and the forceful Reverend Plancius who taught sailors about the stars south of the equator. In 1595, a flotilla of four ships was sent to Asia. The voyage was not a great success. Although the sailors did have some idea of their course, navigation was so primitive that the ships veered off course many times. Also, there was no experience with preserving food and water, and the shortage of fresh vegetables and fruit caused a chronic vitamin deficiency which in turn led to many deaths by the feared scurvy. Another problem was that the sailors were ignorant of the cultures and peoples they encountered, causing recurrent misunderstandings,

quarrels and fights. And if that were not enough, the commanders of the fleet were constantly at odds as well.

After almost a year — the average speed of the ships was about 1.5 knots — the ships reached Bantam. In spite of the resistance offered by the Portuguese who had been doing business in Bantam for more than a century, Cornelis de Houtman, one of the Dutch commanders, succeeded in starting negotiations about deliveries of pepper with the local governor, who was also the guardian of the youthful native king. But because the Dutch stubbornly bid too low, the outcome was disappointing and they were only able to load a small quantity of pepper. The stop in Bantam ended in conflict, and the ships made for eastern Java, but a war between Hindus and Muslims made any landing there impossible. The ships then crossed the straits between Java and Bali, and in spite of strong monsoon winds managed to arrive at what is now Kuta.

After a voyage so full of hardship the sailors were stunned by the beauty of Bali. A deputation of the crew was warmly welcomed by the ruler of Klungkung. The sailors ate pork, watched the beautiful dancers, listened to the *gamelans* which reminded them of church bells in the Netherlands, and they were much impressed by the irrigation systems of the rice fields and the well-organized administration of the island. Two young officers were so impressed that they decided to remain.

Bali and the East India Company

The first voyage to the East Indies was soon followed by more successful ones. The navigators mapped the coastlines and noted the winds, currents, population and trade goods. Enormous profits were made. Dutch merchants from towns such as Amsterdam, Rotterdam, Delft, Hoorn and Enkhuizen, and a group of merchants from the province of Zealand sent ships to take a share of the market. The Portuguese, who had possessed the Asian trade monopoly for more than a century, were furious. England, France and Denmark all envied the Dutch

HOFKER, *Death temple at Batu Bulan Village*, 1938, pastel.

trade successes. Among themselves, the Dutch realized that unification would strengthen their position. This led to a unique enterprise for that time: the East India Company.

The East India Company was the first company to be based on the share principle. It encompassed the five towns and Zealand, who had already organized voyages to Asia. They each had a board, a so-called chamber, which sent representatives to the company's main administration in Amsterdam. The East India Company held the Dutch trade monopoly with Asia. During the East India Company era, which lasted from 1602 to New Year's Eve 1799, the Dutch only occupied the most important trading posts, which were defended by forts for which the bricks as well as the cannon had to be imported from Holland. Batavia, present-day Jakarta, was more than a heavily defended trading post: it was the centre of Dutch administration and there were wharves, quays and warehouses. The important spice islands Ambon (cloves) and Banda

(nutmeg), were also occupied by the Dutch and heavily defended by forts and military posts. The administration and defense were expensive, but the profits of the East India Company were many times higher.

Exotic Prints

From the very first voyages, pictures were fashioned for Europeans of the far lands that the sailors visited. Artistic crew members would sometimes make a sketch and artists back home would make drawings from sailors' tales. The engravings based on such drawings were eagerly purchased: the great majority of people in Europe had never seen palm trees or elephants and tigers, nor did they have any notion of strange peoples and cultures. Due to sailors' exaggerations and fantasies these prints were not always true to life, such as the prints of bizarre monsters, of two-headed people or people hopping on one leg. People could not get enough of the exotic prints. They were copied onto tiles, plates, wood carvings on furniture, and painted onto walls and ceilings. Even clergymen made use of the prints to illustrate the vastness of Creation.

Regrettably, the administrators of the East

11

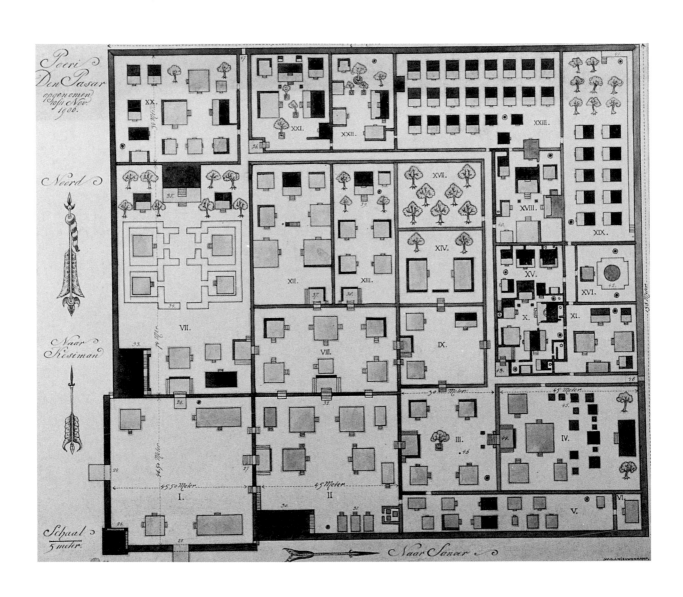

NIEUWENKAMP, *Plan of the puri of Denpasar*, 1906, ink on paper.

IndiaCompany were too parsimonious to spend any money on good artists. Sometimes an artist would sail to the Indies at his own risk to make a living by painting East India Company dignitaries, forts and an occasional landscape. Although the administrators of the East India Company were indifferent to artistic representations of the lands with which they traded, they did show great interest in accurate charts, exact representation of coastlines and, of course, pictures of locally obtainable wares. For that reason, map makers were often sent out to the Indies. The maps would be decorated with bird's eye views of East India Company posts and sometimes they had a high artistic value. However, they were regarded as confidential, and when they were not being used by East India Company captains, they lay locked in the vaults of East India Company offices.

The Colonial Empire Visualised

After the liquidation of the East India Company in 1799, followed by a British administration during the wars with France, the Dutch regained their power in the East Indies. This time they did not only engage in trade, but also in the development of the land. There were explorations for raw materials, rain forests were chopped down on a large scale to make way for plantations. The interior was opened up with roads, bridges and railroads. To be able to administer this enormous area many times the size of the Netherlands, an extensive administrative network of civil servants was set up. Local rulers received positions in the colonial hierarchy in exchange for various rights. Missionaries were sent to the most remote areas to convert the population. Because of the demand for encyclopedic knowledge which arose at the end of the eighteenth century the whole of Indonesia, including various cultural manifestations, was being depicted by travelling draughtsmen. These activities resulted in an enormous collection of drawings of landscapes, villages, native costumes, utensils and the like. In the course of the nineteenth century this work was gradually taken over by photographers.

Resistance on Bali

In the first decades of the nineteenth century there was strong resistance against the Dutch in Indonesia. The Dutch felt that their authority was being undermined by the rather intensive contacts between Bali and Singapore. Chinese and Buginese sailed their small but seaworthy craft up and down between Bali and Singapore and other destinations, freely trading in goods such as opium, rice, textiles, meat, gunpowder and arms and imported the *kepeng*, Chinese coins with a square hole in the middle, which were used as official tender on Bali.

The Dutch did not like this free trade, nor did they like the British using the island as a stop on the passage to Australia and as a means of extending their influence on Java. Another source of irritation for the Dutch was the *tawang karang*, the ancient right to any ship that went down off the coast of Bali. In the course of the 1840s the Dutch therefore sought to sway the rulers of Bali. By giving gifts, the Raja of Klungkung for example was honoured with a white rhinoceros, the Dutch attempted to force the rulers to transfer sovereignty.

Misunderstandings and cultural differences resulted in a military expedition organized by the Dutch government. A fairly strong force of 62 ships and 3,000 men was sent to Bali in June, 1846. The soldiers landed on the North coast and destroyed Buleleng and Singaraja. After negotiations in which it was agreed that the Balinese were to submit to Dutch authority, the troops withdrew. However, since in the view of the Dutch nothing really changed, a new force was sent out in 1848. The Balinese were able to muster 15,000 men; the Dutch were lured into an ambush and lost face in the entire East Indies. In 1849 a new expedition was sent out. This time the campaign ended in a settlement mediated by the Danish merchant Mads Lange who had his offices in Kuta. Again it was agreed that the Balinese rulers would recognize Dutch suzerainty.

NIEUWENKAMP

The *Sri Kulama* Disaster

On May 27, 1904 the Dutch-registered schooner *Sri Kumala* stranded on the notorious reef off the coast of Sanur. The captain, a man called Kwee Tek Tjiang from Banjarmasin (Borneo), was able to bring a part of the cargo of trasi, sugar and *kepeng* onto the beach. By the next morning most of it had been stolen, and the wreck on the reef had been thoroughly plundered. The furious captain made a complaint to the *punggawa*, the district chief, who shrugged and referred to the *tawan karang*.

In desperation, Captain Kwee brought the matter to the attention of the Dutch authorities. Resident Esbach listened to the captain's account and foresaw great problems for the normally tranquil island. He was right; the incident was the first act of a drama. When the

Left: NIEUWENKAMP, *Village in Karangasem*, 1937, pencil drawing.

complaint reached Batavia, Governor General van Heutz, whose name was feared after his bloody subjugation of Aceh, decided that it was time for rebellious Bali to be brought under direct Dutch rule.

The *Puputan*

The shipwreck of 1904 was used as a reason to put matters right. After an increasingly acrimonious correspondence between the governor general in Batavia and the Balinese rulers a military expedition was sent to Bali. After landing in Kusamba the soldiers marched to the *puri* (palace) of the Raja of Badung, near Denpasar, under whose jurisdiction Sanur lay. The morning of September 20, 1906 would not be easily forgotten by the hardened soldiers of the Royal Netherlands Indies Army (KNIL)

The Raja knew that his downfall was inevitable. Instead of ignominious defeat he chose *puputan* (ritual suicide) for himself and his entire court. When the heavily armed KNIL soldiers had reached the palace, they were surprised to see the Raja appear in full ceremonial costume, seated in his sedan chair and surrounded by his wives and children. Everyone wore ceremonial dress as if they were on their way to a temple feast. In spite of warnings and shots in the air, the procession continued to make its way to the soldiers who then shot to kill. A massacre ensued. The Balinese who were not shot down used their *krisses* (daggers) to kill first the wounded around them and then themselves. Moments later the road was strewn with the corpses of men, women and children. The soldiers ravaged the area, collected the jewels and other precious items and without much resistance from the local population they occupied a number of strategic points. Eventually, the Dutch reinstated their authority, but in a way no general could be proud of and which caused much criticism in their home country.

The Artist on the Bicycle

The Dutch artist W.O.J. Nieuwenkamp witnessed the bloodshed on Bali. He had visited Bali earlier in 1903 and he had published the drawings he had made then at his own expense. Nieuwenkamp's was dismayed about the *puputan* and extremely annoyed about the behaviour of the soldiers who thoughtlessly destroyed temples and palaces and chopped up beautifully carved *gamelan* supports to use them for their cooking fires. But he also realized he could not criticize the Governor General's policies. His report in a Dutch newspaper of the *puputan* of the court of the Raja of Badung was restrained. His indignation does surface in surviving letters to his wife with passages such as:

'I have not yet decided whether I should write the Handelsblad (a Dutch newspaper) about the war here. I am certain that what I have to say will not coincide with the official embellished telegrams, and with those

Above: *Stone relief on the temple of Medoewe Karang, depicting Nieuwenkamp on his bicycle.*
Left: NIEUWENKAMP, *Landing of the Dutch troops at Sanur in 1906*, published in Nieuwenkamp's *Bali en Lombok*, 1910.

letters I will make many enemies here. I am very curious to see what the papers will make of the investiture of Denpasar, the main town, whether they will turn it into a heroic feat.' And also: 'In the entire campaign so far we have lost only four men, proof that there never was any real fighting, just a horrible massacre.'

Nieuwenkamp was assigned a space under the gallery of the *puri*, where he could bivouac under the protection of the troops. But he preferred an improvised rag hut in the burned ruins of a house. While the soldiers did not set foot out of their camp, Nieuwenkamp used his bicycle to reconnoitre the beauty of Bali far from the chaos of war.

Travel

Wijnand Otto Jan Nieuwenkamp was born in Amsterdam on July 17, 1874 to a merchant and shipowner whose ships brought in, among other things, spices from the Moluccas. Although Nieuwenkamp's father would have liked his son to become a clergyman, young Wijnand soon indicated that he wished to become an artist. At the gymnasium he was a difficult student who preferred to give his time to drawing and to his cousin Anna with whom he had fallen in love. After a number of failed attempts, father Nieuwenkamp gave up on his son in 1895, and Nieuwenkamp junior proceeded to attempt to make a living by making illustrations. Nieuwenkamp drew detailed town scenes and started to specialize in the precise technique of etching.

As a writer for a magazine, he voyaged to the Indies for the first time in 1898 and visited Batavia, Jogyakarta and Bandung. This trip resulted in a flood of drawings. The drawings of Bandung were published in a guidebook by the famous Homan Hotel. After working for some years in the Netherlands and Germany, Nieuwenkamp again went to the Indies in 1903 and on that occasion he stopped on Bali. He felt at home there, as it appears from the letter announcing his arrival: 'I am on Bali now, and I like it very well, what a divine place, constant fine weather, constant sunshine, never too hot, because the stroke of flat land is very narrow and the cold mountain air mingles with the cool sea breeze. Very picturesque, beautiful trees, beautiful mountains, beautiful beach, beautiful temples, nice people, in short a delightful place, a small paradise. And also very cheap for me.'

Pristine Bali

When Nieuwenkamp was on Bali, the island was not yet a tourist destination. In the North, at Singaraja, there were the offices and warehouses of a handful of merchants and administrators. In the South, the ships anchored off the fishing village Sanur. The civil servants were stationed to the North in Denpasar. There were few roads and the mountains formed a sharp division between North and South. Due to the lack of communication between the various domains there were major cultural differences.

When Nieuwenkamp came to Bali for the first time, the island was divided into nine realms and society was divided into four castes. In the course of the centuries the influence of Islam had gradually pushed the ancient Hindu court culture of the great Majapahit dynasty to East Java but on the isolated island Bali it had remained almost unchanged. Rituals and ceremonies were usually accompanied by dance, music and numerous decorations, which always provided work for the artistic craftsmen who often lived together in groups so that there were villages of smiths, painters, woodcarvers or sculptors. Nieuwenkamp feared, as did the artists and scholars who visited the island after him, that western influences would quickly make the ancient Hindu traditions disappear. This drove him to work frenziedly at recording everything he saw: feasts and ceremonies, people at work, landscapes and buildings.

Nieuwenkamp remained above all an illustrator. He did not participate in contemporary developments in West European painting. At most, the influence of *Jugendstil* can sometimes be discerned in his drawings. Through his family and his marriage Nieuwenkamp was well-off and was able to devote himself entirely to his great hobby, drawing anything that interested him.

Bali in a Book

Nieuwenkamp's first voyage to Bali resulted in so many drawings and information that he decided to publish a beautifully edited book at his own expense. It was received enthusiastically and since Nieuwenkamp had liked Bali so much, he decided to return to collect material for a second volume. Nieuwenkamp succeeded in describing Balinese culture before it, as he feared, was changed by western influences.

Nieuwenkamp made various voyages in Asia. In 1917 he returned to Bali and saw the damage that had been done by the great earthquake of September 17 and also that the new roads and bridges had greatly changed the island. In 1937 he visited Bali for the last

time. During that visit he concentrated on architecture, which resulted in the appearance in 1947 of the book *Architecture and Sculpture on Bali*. Since 1926 Nieuwenkamp and his wife had mostly been living in their Italian villa near Florence. Nieuwenkamp died there on April 23, 1950.

Above: NIEUWENKAMP, *Cock fighting theatre in Bangli*, 1905, drawing.

NIEUWENKAMP, *Funeral*,
drawing.

NIEUWENKAMP, *Funeral procession
in Sangsit*, 1922, drawing.

NIEUWENKAMP, *Tabanan, bamboo copy of a KLM airoplane*, 1937, drawing.

NIEUWENKAMP, *Temple gate in
a village in Gianyar*, 1922,
drawing.

Above: NIEUWENKAMP,
River crossing in south Bali, 1907,
etching.
Left: NIEUWENKAMP, *landscape,
Jimbaran*, drawing.

Above: NIEUWENKAMP, *Sawahs in the mountains*, 1904, drawing.
Right above: NIEUWENKAMP, *Temple gate in Sangsit*, 1910, woodcut.
Right below: NIEUWENKAMP, *Cemetery on Bali*, 1904, woodcut.

Above: NIEUWENKAMP, *Besakih*, 1937, drawing.
Right: NIEUWENKAMP, *Balinese dancer*, 1937, drawing.

Left above: NIEUWENKAMP, *The Batur Temple, drawing made in 1904 — the temple was destroyed after a volcanic eruption in 1905 and a subsequent earthquake in 1917*, 1904, drawing.
Left below: NIEUWENKAMP, *The Puri of Karangasem*, 1910, drawing.
Above: NIEUWENKAMP, *The 'Moon of Pejeng' bronze drum*, 1906, drawing.
Right: NIEUWENKAMP, *Goa Gajah (the elephant cave) in Gianyar*, 1925, drawing.

Above: NIEUWENKAMP, *Market scene*, 1937, drawing.
Left above: NIEUWENKAMP, *Village scene in Selat*, 1918, drawing.
Left below: NIEUWENKAMP, *Gamelan orchestra, Selat*, 1937, drawing.

Above and left: NIEUWENKAMP,
Depictions of famous Balinese
fairy tales, 1910, drawings.

BONNET

Bali as Museum

The colonial government in Batavia was at a loss what to do after the *puputans*. While Bali had been brought under colonial rule, this had not taken place after bloody man-to-man fights as in Aceh. Instead, some rajas had chosen death for themselves and their families and retinue. The rest of the population continued their lives as if nothing had happened. The few artists, scientists and civil servants who were allowed to stay on the island all sang its praises.

Gregor Krause, a famous German physician and anthropologist working for the Dutch colonial administration was full of admiration for the manner in which children were raised. In an article published in a magazine in 1918 he wrote: 'Nowhere else in the world does one see children raised that are so agreeable, so eager

Left: BONNET, *Pencak dance*, 1934, pastel.

to learn, so trusting, and as well-behaved as the parents. And where is the country where, without schools, almost everyone learns to read and write, where small boys draw figures in the sand and on walls, which are envied by many of us calling ourselves artists? Where else do little girls braid temple hangers from *lontar* leaves and flowers and bring their little gifts to the temple where they pray as devoutly as their marvellous mothers?' Krause thought Balinese culture should be changed as little as possible, an opinion with which the Dutch administration came to agree.

The government even went so far as to prohibit missionaries from spreading Christianity, as this would have taken the soul out of Balinese culture. This was a measure which the churches did not appreciate: 'our activities at this post have been much curtailed', a certain Father Kersten wrote from Denpasar. 'Taking care of the spiritual needs of the small group of European Catholics did not take much time. We were not permitted to religiously influence the native population, and the local government saw to it that the limits of our

Left: BONNET, *Portrait of a boy*, 1929, pastel.
Below, from left to right: BONNET, *Portrait of a boy*, 1931; *Portrait of a Young man*, 1948; *Portrait of a woman*, 1929, pastel.

activities were not even remotely reached. These restrictions were effective, and the reports that went to Batavia were numerous. It appeared that Bali's time had not yet come.'

Other measures were taken to protect the culture and monuments. In administration circles a plan was made to start a museum in Denpasar. In 1914 at the request of the colonial government the Dutch author Augusta de Wit detailed the plan in a report: 'This work of civilization is, of course, in its infancy. The Assistant Resident of Bandung has made a plan — which has been agreed to by all *puggawas* of the areas under direct rule as well as by the 'self-governments' — to found a museum in Den Pasar, a complex of buildings that will be a model of Balinese architecture and a treasure house of Balinese Art. Each part of the island will have its own building in its own fashion, its own style of utensils for daily use and the products of its industry will be exhibited. It will not be a dead collection of this and that. The adjoining temple will be as open for use as any *pura* (*puri*) and the great bath will be equipped for daily use. The proceeds of objects put up for sale will serve for maintenance, and foreign visitors may be expected.'

The monument conservationist P.R.J. Moojen, who received the assignment of making an inventory of the damage caused by the volcanic eruption of 1918, urged the restoration of temples and palaces by using sensible bricks and roof tiles instead of the traditional materials. Moojen also made a fiery appeal to avoid the usual uniform architecture of government buildings and to employ the traditional architecture of the island instead. It was not realized, however, that Balinese culture was based on an ancient cycle of creation and loss; boys and girls were continually educated to pass on that tradition. The Dutch colonial government wished to protect the island in its own way by conserving the culture, not realizing that in this way the development of centuries would be brought to a standstill and that craftmanship would be lost.

Traditional Painting

Artists such as Rudolf Bonnet and Walter Spies chose an entirely different approach. They wished to stimulate development by carefully introducing Western elements alongside traditional ways. However, it would be wrong to suppose that without Spies and Bonnet, Balinese art would have remained the same up to the present. On the contrary, it is the vigour of Balinese art that allows it to renew itself in its own way after absorbing outside influences. Besides the many talented artists that were able to absorb outside influences into tradition, there were a number of gifted artists such as I Gusti Nyoman Leopad, who created original innovations from existing forms of art.

It should also be mentioned that Balinese painting did not have an equivalent ranking in the arts as compared to painting in the West. Dance was and is the most exalted art form for the Balinese, it is a way of experiencing religion and the link between everyday life and the timeless affairs of the hereafter. Next in importance after dance comes the music which is so closely associated with it. For example, the *gamelans* are constructed, consecrated and played with a devotion that is totally alien to western music. A simpler form of visualizing old Hindu myths such as the *Ramayana* and the *Mahabharata* is the *wayang* theatre which is also accompanied by the *gamelan*. Next there are the religious as well as decorative arts such as making various types of textiles, wood carving, sculpting and finally painting.

Painted textiles were used as decoration for ceremonial beds and important chambers or were hung up for important occasions. Also, painted panels were used for ceremonial beds or on the ceilings of buildings with a special purpose such as the pavilion in the palace of the Klungkung where justice was done. It is to the credit of Bonnet and Spies, and later Arie Smit, that painting has risen in the hierarchy of Balinese art.

The composition and depiction of traditional paintings were bound to strict rules. The illustrated figures were just like the *wayang*, not representations of everyday humans, but stereotypes with certain characteristics, such as stance and shape of the eyes, posture, colours and clothing, which made them instantly recognizable to an audience. By relative positioning on the paintings, ranks were denoted and a distinction made between gods and demons. Things such as a fire, a village, a forest or the sea were suggested by simple symbols.

The knowledge about making traditional paintings was passed on in *lontar* books. These were palm leaf books in which figures were portrayed by incisions with a sharp knife daubed with a mixture of soot and oil. The fragility of these works made it necessary to constantly replace old *lontar* books, so that they constantly needed to be copied and redrawn. This process by itself was part of continually passing on ancient knowledge and technique. When contacts with the west had apparently created a demand for such things, Rudolf Bonnet was able to persuade Balinese artists to render scenes from everyday life besides those in myths, portraying human figures with a realistic rather than symbolic anatomy.

Rudolf Bonnet

Rudolf Bonnet was born in Amsterdam in 1895, on no. 2 Jodenbreestraat, across from the house where Rembrandt had lived at the apex of his fame. Rudolf was a quiet boy, who lived in a fantasy world and most of all wished to develop his talent for drawing. His father, a self-made man who had climbed from humble schoolteacher to businessman and property owner, saw no future in this. Especially due to the efforts of his mother, Rudolf finally did get his father's permission to attend art school, on the condition that he would specialize in design, so that he would be able to make a living. At the age of 21, Bonnet began his career as an independent artist. He drew portraits with the diligence and tenacity which would characterize his whole life.

In 1920 Rudolf Bonnet journeyed to Italy with his parents. The southern country with its hotblooded people, so different from calvinist Holland, was a revelation to Bonnet, the outcome of which was an enormous production of drawings of people, villages, and landscapes. He soon returned to Italy and worked in a rented studio for months. In the meantime in the Netherlands his work was exhibited with success sever-

al times and the young artist started to make his name. In Rome he met W.O.J. Nieuwenkamp, who advised him to visit Bali. But first Bonnet crossed the Mediterranean to look around in North Africa.

The Mediterranean

In the sixteenth and seventeenth centuries it had been the wish of many Dutch artists to travel to Italy to become engrossed in and inspired by the remnants of Roman culture. Once they were back in the Netherlands, their paintings had become infused with light and colour, the influence of the South which so many Dutch artists have felt. However, by the nineteenth century Dutch painters' urge to travel had virtually disappeared.

While the French Impressionists sought their inspiration around the Mediterranean, the Dutch painters stayed home. Dutch art in Bonnet's time was primarily set in the Netherlands, favouring rainy town scenes, and grey skies over whitecapped waves. Artists such as Nieuwenkamp were the exception to the rule. Bonnet's Italian and North African work immediately drew favourable attention amid the Dutch landscapes and town scenes. As soon as the proceeds from his paintings were sufficient to make him independent of his father, Bonnet packed his suitcases and voyaged to Bali.

Ubud

In 1929 Bonnet arrived on Bali. After a hesitant start — he was tired and fell ill for a while — his interest for the island grew, especially after he had seen a Balinese dance for the first time. He met Walter Spies, the German artist who had arrived two years earlier and Jaap Kunst, the Dutch musicologist who was one of the first westerners to make a study of *gamelan* music. Bonnet travelled to Nias with Kunst; where he drew and photographed, returned to Bali in 1930 and settled in Ubud. He moved into a pavilion in the middle of a pond across from the *puri* of the art-loving ruler Cokorde Gde Agung Sukawati.

Above: BONNET, *Djemoel*, undated,
pastel.
Right: BONNET, *I Tjemul*, 1949,
pastel.

Individual Art

Any Saturday in 1937 was strangely busy at Rudolf
Bonnet's house. Inside, a group of Balinese and
Dutchmen would be waiting. They were the selection
committee of the *Pita Maha*, a society for Balinese art
started by art gallery owners. Outside the house the
artists would be walking up, from Ubud, Batuan,
Penestanan, Sanur and other places. They would have
taken their new paintings along for rating by the committee. These artists belonged to the select group
whose work had been found good enough to be sold
in a number of art galleries on Bali and to be sent to
exhibitions elsewhere in the Indies, in the Netherlands
and even in the United States. The artists were flattered
that their work had been found good enough to be
shown off the island, and the recognition of the *Pita
Maha* also gave them a fairly regular income.

The *Pita Maha* was a well-intentioned but totally
western affair contrary to the Asian way of creating art.
Through the centuries western art had become an
increasingly individual affair. Towards the end of the
nineteenth century, some artists felt that art should be
the most individual expression of the most individual
emotion. While an artist might have ties to a group, a
trend, or a school of art, his work of art was an individual expression, signed with his own name as a safe-
guard against forgery. In this way, a sold painting still,
in a way, remained the property of its maker.

Oriental art had a mainly religious function. The
idea was primarily to deliver an optimum product. Who
the artist was was not most important. Often various
artists would work on a single painting. One of them,
with knowledge of the tales that were to be depicted
and with a feeling for composition would make the
sketch, others would fill in the colours, and finally an

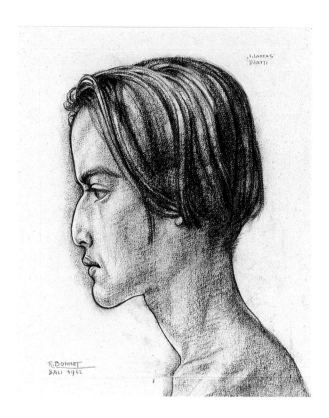

BONNET, *I Lantas*, 1952, pastel.

experienced professional would add the colour accentuations and shadow lines. They would inspect each others' work and try to copy good examples as exactly as possible. A painting was the work of a collective and therefore was not signed by an individual.

In descriptions of the *Pita Maha*, there are usually extensive accounts of changed technique and composition. But the individualization caused by the *Pita Maha* was much more drastic; it was in fact unknown to Balinese culture. Balinese artists began to depict their own fantasies in their own way, and no longer adhered to the tradition of following each other's examples.

Changes

No matter how much it was attempted by a small group of intellectuals and artists, Bali could not be isolated from the rest of the world, nor could it be turned into a vast open air museum. Roads and bridges were built, more visitors came, including more curious artists. Previously, the few external influences had been absorbed into Balinese art. In the years between the world wars, Bali was flooded by new impressions brought in by modern means of communication and transport. Turning back that flood was impossible, and it was more interesting to ascertain whether Balinese art was vigorous enough to absorb the stream of impressions and to renew itself.

Pita Maha

Before Spies' and Bonnet's arrival the tranquillity of Bali had already been disturbed. Balinese artists had observed the first tourists and their behaviour and had incorporated that into their art. Nieuwenkamp was a good example: he was depicted with his bicycle. This was followed by depictions of western tourists in their cars, with cameras and other attributes. The interest of tourists in Balinese art quickly gave shrewd entrepreneurs the idea to work commercially. Cokorde Gde Agung Sukawati thought he might enrich the art in his city and he invited Spies to come and live in Ubud. While Spies' fear was that traditions would be lost, Bonnet did not worry that artists would end up assembling quick and cheap gewgaws for the tourists.

Originally, good-quality art that had the approval of experts was sold at the Bali Museum in Denpasar. But when gallery owners started to complain about the, as they saw it, unfair competition, sales at the museum were stopped and in 1936 the *Pita Maha* (Great Spirit, Guiding Inspiration) was founded. The board consisted of Cokorde Gde Agung Sukawati and the painters I Gusti Nyoman Lempad, Spies and Bonnet.

For a number of years the shop of the Neuhaus brothers in Sanur was an important outlet for selected works of art. These German brothers combined their interest in nature with business instinct. For the first tourists they had already built a sea aquarium. This tourist attraction was soon expanded with Balinese statues several metres high and an art shop, which included the works of the *Pita Maha*.

The years just before the Second World War were difficult for the *Pita Maha*. Spies was convicted of indecent behaviour and when shortly thereafter he was expelled from the *Pita Maha*, Bonnet also left. Soon after that, the war broke out. Spies was interned and was killed during transportation. Bonnet was taken prisoner by the Japanese in 1942, and with other Dutch nationals, including the painter Willem Hofker, he ended up in a prison camp near Makasar (Ujung Pandang).

In 1947 Bonnet returned to Bali. In Campuan near Ubud he built his *Kesume Girit* (Flower Hill), a house and studio of bamboo built according to Balinese tradition. It was a time with few tourists: there was increasing tension between the Republic of Indonesia that had been proclaimed in 1945, and the Netherlands government which intended to restore the prewar colony. There was almost nothing left of the fashionable set of foreigners and their visitors from the twenties and thirties. There were no patronizing Dutch civil servants and no pressure from art dealers. The artists were able to work without hindrance. More than before the war, Bonnet increasingly blended in with the people of Bali. He was a member of the dea associations and was asked for advice in all sorts of things. In the meantime, with few interruptions from visitors, he rapidly worked on. His drawings were quick and true; examples are

the swift sketches of monkeys and parrots. His few oils are sometimes too elaborate, which makes them somewhat static. But he was a master in chalk and pastel drawings; especially the portraits of Balinese boys excelled in their subdued tenderness, which made Bonnet's love for Bali and its people almost palpable.

Bonnet was popular on Bali, with the painters as well as with the models. People admired his work, although Bonnet himself tended to be modest and was always striving for improvement of his technique. When one of his models asked what he would like to be in a next life, Bonnet answered : 'Painter, but with more talent'. Although Bonnet guarded against influencing the Balinese too heavily — at the most, he would provide some instruction in the depiction of anatomy — he was so highly regarded that the Balinese artists paid him the highest compliment of imitating his work as carefully as they could. Although

Below left: BONNET, *Pan Mante*,
1930s, crayon.
Below: BONNET, *Figure of a man*,
1950, oil on canvas.

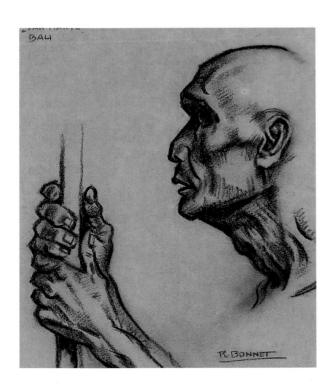

there were painters who returned to Balinese traditions and matured in that direction, there was a large group of followers of Bonnet who developed an odd style with Balinese scenes of cock fights, *pasars* and *sawahs*, filled with figures in the style of Bonnet. To this day there are painters who pass on this instantly recognizable way of painting from father to son.

Puri Lukisan

Although the *Pita Maha* had been disbanded, Bonnet continued to do its work. He selected high-quality work for exhibitions and worked to found a museum of Balinese art. Together with Cokorde Gde Agung Sukawati, Bonnet succeeded in accomplishing this goal in 1954. In Ubud the construction was started of the *Puri Lukisan*, the palace of paintings, according to Bonnet's design. The museum consisted of a roomy main hall in the Balinese style, which was reached through a fairytale garden with a lotus pond. In the

museum a part of Bonnet's collection was exhibited, supplemented with gifts.

In the meantime relations between the Netherlands and Indonesia had deteriorated. The Netherlands sent in troops to suppress the Republic. This did not, however, stop Bonnet from executing his plans. He had become too old to be called up and also he was fortunate enough to have fallen into President Sukarno's good graces. The Indonesian President started a large art collection which included fourteen of Bonnet's works. In the course of the fifties the remaining Dutch in Indonesia were put under increasing pressure to leave the country. Bonnet was expelled after a refusal to finish a portrait of Sukarno, and to the regret of many Balinese Bonnet left for the Netherlands in 1957. He journeyed on to Anticoli in Italy and from there made several trips to North Africa, and in 1963 he finally settled in the Netherlands.

Many attempts were made to get Bonnet back to Indonesia. Cokorde Gde Agung Sukawati made efforts to finish the *Puri Lukasan* museum together with Bonnet. However, due to red tape and politics, Bonnet was not able to return to Bali for some months until 1972, when he helped expand the museum and organized an opening exhibition. He was satisfied and touched to discover that he had not been forgotten, and in the media he was hailed as the returned spiritual father and teacher of many Balinese artists.

Bonnet would return to Bali several times. He organized exhibitions, painted, drew and taught. In the Netherlands Bonnet organized exhibitions of Indonesian art, for which at that time there was only limited interest. On April 18, 1978 Bonnet passed away after a long illness. He was cremated, and at the request of his Balinese friends his ashes were brought to Bali, where an exceptional tribute was paid to his memory when his ashes were burnt together with the body of his friend Cokorde Gde Agung Sukawati in a great traditional ceremony on January 31, 1981.

Left: BONNET, *Ngoenjing, kris dance*, 1934, pastel.
Right: BONNET, *Grass cutter*, 1936, ink and pastel.

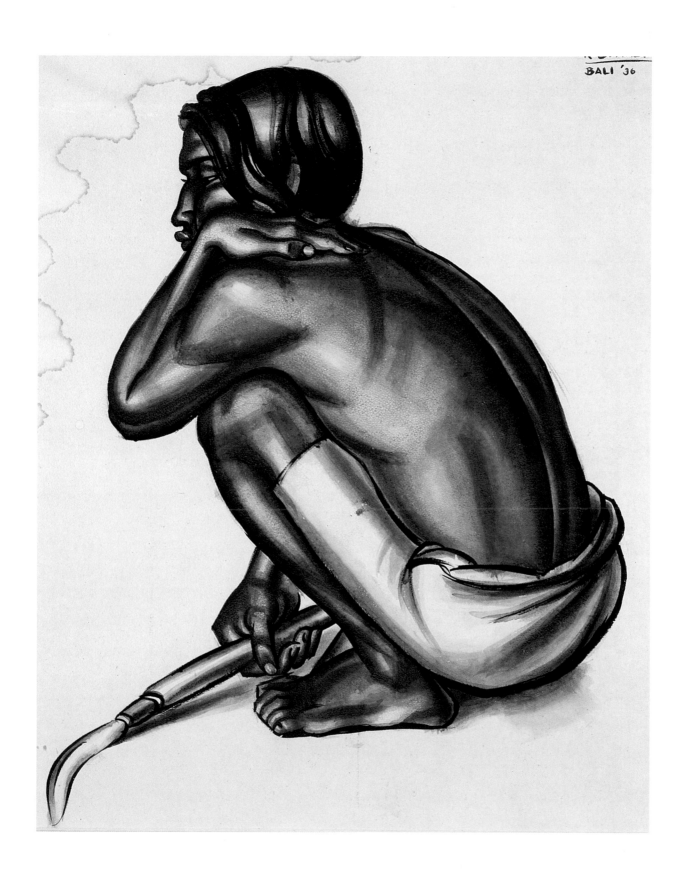

Above: BONNET, *Two men resting*,
1940, pastel.
Left: BONNET, *Sleeping man*, 1938,
pastel.

Above: BONNET, *Dewa Nooman,
Makassar*, 1940, pastel.
Right: BONNET, *Portrait of a
Javanese man, Jogyakarta*, 1937,
pastel.

JOGJA 1937

R. BONNET

Above: BONNET, *Men hoeing*, 1940,
gouache, pastel and charcoal.
Left: BONNET, *Sketches of parrots
and monkeys*, n.d., crayon.
Right: BONNET, *Poera Dalem,
Ubud*, 1947, pastel.

51

Above: BONNET, *Portrait of a young man*, 1931, pastel.
Left: BONNET, *Ramin*, 1931, pastel.
Right: BONNET, *Two men*, 1975, pastel.

SPIES

Tourists

The First World War was a traumatic experience for many Europeans. Millions of young lives had been destroyed and confidence in western culture was seriously weakened. The twenties were characterized by attempts to forget, through escapes to other cultures, and by fascination with exotic religions. Bali conformed well to the age. It offered the dazed westerner the harmony and satisfaction which in Europe had been replaced by battlefields. Bali became a popular destination due to tourists who spread the island's fame, at the same time wishing to keep the paradise they had discovered for themselves. Commerce quickly made use of the demand for exotic destinations. Voyages to Bali were made by the Royal Dutch Steam Packet Company (KPM), which anchored off the coast at

Left: SPIES, *River landscape*,
undated, oil on canvas.

Buleleng. Except for the occasional civil servant or merchant, the steamers usually picked up pigs, which were plentiful on Bali. The pigs were floated to the ships on rafts and hoisted aboard, with much squealing, by means of 'trousers'. They were exported to Javanese ports and to Singapore. Because of the pigs the KPM run to Bali was nicknamed the 'Babi-express'.

In 1922 and 1924 the steamers *Van der Wijck* and *Plancius* were taken into service. These liners had good passenger accommodations and their Makasar-Surabaya-Palembang run included a stop at Bali. Tourists would be offloaded in small boats on the North coast which would take them through the surf, after which helpful Balinese would carry them onto dry land. After spending the night in Singaraja they would travel to Denpasar by car along the winding mountain roads. In 1925 the famous and chique Bali Hotel was opened in Denpasar. In 1930 there were about a hundred tourists a year — ten years later that number had increased to about 250. For most tourists, just as for tourists in the present day, their stay on Bali was a five-day arrangement consisting of a trip by car from Singaraja to Denpasar and a stay in Denpasar with, at the most, some excursions to nearby temples or the coastal village Sanur. The program included a *rijsttafel* ('rice table', a sumptuous meal of many Indonesian dishes) and dance performances. The number of tourists — most of them wealthy — was sufficient to start a small tourist industry. Painters and wood carvers started to produce paintings and wooden sculptures that would be attractive to tourists and which could be transported easily.

Besides the tourists seeking adventure or distraction there were the artists and scholars who wished to learn about Balinese culture. They avoided the tourists, settled among the population for longer periods of time and interpreted the culture surrounding them from their own points of view. During the twenties and thirties there was a fashionable artistic and somewhat decadent circle of westerners. For a long time the German artist Walter Spies was its central figure.

An Artist of Many Talents

Walter Spies was born in Moscow on September 15, 1895, the son of a German diplomatic family. In contrast to Bonnet, he grew up in an intellectual and artistic environment. From an early age he showed a great interest in nature, music, dance and painting. He easily learned foreign languages, and he quickly mastered the choreography of exotic dances. He quickly became accustomed to oriental music. Usually he did not take the time for writing or painting. At age fifteen, to complete his education he was sent to Dresden. As young as he was, he became absorbed in the modern art forms which could be seen and heard in Dresden, which was then one of the major European art centres. He saw the experimental work of cubist and expressionist artists and listened to the music of Richard Strauss.

Both world wars strongly gave direction to Spies' life and at the same time gave him the chance to show his vitality and vigour up to his death in 1942. The First World war broke out when Spies was vacationing with his parents in Moscow. Spies' father was interned with the other Germans. For a year Walter helped his mother nurse the wounded in their large house in Moscow. But as soon as he reached age twenty and was eligible for military service, he was also sent to a camp, far away in the Urals. This did not depress Spies — he enjoyed the countryside, listened to the music and melancholy songs of the Tartars and Khirgiz and amazed friends and enemies with his perfect performances of Russian dances. During the confusion of the Russian Revolution, Spies returned to Moscow and then to Germany to rejoin his family who had gone back there in the meantime.

Dresden

Back in Germany, Walter Spies became absorbed in the blossoming cultural atmosphere in the years after the First World war. In Dresden he met the painters Oskar Kokoschka and Otto Dix. He admired the work of Marc Chagall, traded thoughts with composers such as Paul Hindemuth and Arthur Schnabel and surprised the people around him with his virtuosity on the piano.

In the summer of 1919 he presented his first paintings at an exhibition and immediately received recognition and praise. Soon after, he left for Berlin and devoted himself to motion pictures and musicals. Sometimes he would make his escape from the booming Berlin of the twenties to the island of Sylt or he would visit his Dutch friends, the conductor Schoonderbeek, famous for his performances of Bach, and his wife. He admired the modern art exhibitions in The Hague and Amsterdam, had his own exhibition, and in the Amsterdam Tropical Museum he was introduced to objects and pictures from the Netherlands East Indies. Slowly his environment became oppressive to him; he desired to leave Europe and to seek unknown faraway places. In 1923 he made his decision and boarded a ship for Java.

Right: SPIES, *Village on the Dieng Plateau, Java*, 1924, oil on canvas.

In the *Kraton*

After an uneventful voyage Spies arrived in Batavia and from there took the train to Bandung. In a lyrical letter to his mother, Walter described the Indies, where he felt at home immediately. He admired the people he would paint so often in later years, for their beauty and natural grace. 'The people, the Sundanese and the Javanese, are so incredibly beautiful, so delicately built, brown and aristocratic, that everyone who is not one of them should be ashamed', he wrote in Bandung. Spies was less complementary about the Dutch: 'The Dutch here are the most hateful and small-minded people that one can imagine, uncivilized, haughty, stupid, bored, arrogant. I cannot find the words to express how I despise them'. Spies effortlessly learned Malay as well as the Javanese court language. From the beginning he was struck by *gamelan* music, the court dances and the songs. From Bandung, Spies journeyed to Jogyakarta. There he landed in two worlds. To earn a

living he played the piano in the band at the Dutch club *De Vereniging* ('The Association') on the *Alun-Alun* near the residential palace. But Spies' heart was at the other side of the square, where the sultan lived, surrounded by his many wives, children and servants and a western orchestra, as well as the most beautiful and largest *gamelan* ensemble in Indonesia.

As a guest at the sultan's parties, one evening Spies found himself in the *kraton*, the sultan's court. He was enchanted by the dancing and the *gamelan* music; these aroused passions in him reminiscent of those during the performance of Bach's Mattheuspassion in the Netherlands. The sultan was struck by how different Spies' reaction to the music was compared to the other nonchalant Europeans. He asked questions about the blond German and a few days later a carriage with princes and servants with *pajongs* stopped in front of Spies' humble boarding house. He was asked to become the conductor of the European orchestra in the *kraton*. Eagerly he assented and he received a pavilion in the *kraton* to live in. His wages were a hundred guilders a month plus food and rent and a young servant. Spies also conducted a choir and gave piano lessons.

SPIES, *Preanger landscape, Java,*
1923, oil on canvas.

In 1925 Walter Spies participated in a group exhibition in Surabaya, with some dreamy landscapes, including the famous painting *The Crab Fishermen*. In that painting, Spies shook off Chagall's influence, with his characters floating through the air, as well as Rousseau's naive style. *The Crab Fishermen* utilizes a bird's eye view which is typical of Spies, to catch people in a beautiful environment going about everyday matters.

But Spies was more interested in the music and dance in the *kraton* than in painting. He could not get enough of seeing the elegant dancers move like 'Egyptian princesses' and was disgusted by the contrast when he was required to pound a foxtrot on the piano and watch the fat Dutch masses whirl around. Spies created a real masterpiece when he rendered a western interpretation of Javanese music. To the surprise of the Javanese he was then able to produce *gamelan* music on pianos which were tuned to the Javanese scale. The enthusiasm in the *kraton* was boundless when he arranged a piece in which the accompaniment for traditional Javanese song and dance was alternately played by a piano and the *gamelan* orchestra.

Spies thought he was in paradise and enjoyed every day of it. He thought he had found a place of absolute beauty, until a first visit to Bali in 1925 made him even more enthusiastic. For a month he travelled around the island, talked to priests, rulers and craftsmen and was amazed at the continual cycle of rituals and ceremonies which were more mysterious than those he was used to on Java. Breathlessly he watched the small girls in their beautiful clothes being carried around in trance, and was astounded by the rhythm and the singing of the men performing war dances. 'I hope to return for a longer period of time', he wrote 'because to me there seems to be no end to Bali'.

Campuan

Bali stayed in Spies' mind. In 1927 he no longer resisted temptation and asked the Sultan of Jogyakarta to relieve him of his position and left for Bali, where he was hospitably received by the *Panggawa* of Ubud, Cokorde Gde Agung Sukawati. Until he was taken away for internment in 1942, Spies remained on Bali, spending the larger part of his life there. He moved to the so-called Water Palace, a house across from the *puri* of the ruler, and a year later he built a house in Campuan, where he found the peace and space to work on painting, photography and music. Spies became absorbed in various aspects of Balinese culture, as was expressed in his drawings, articles about music, and especially his photographs which soon became well-known all over the world.

Together with the Dutch anthropologist Roelof Goris he wrote a book about Bali in 1931, commissioned by the Royal Dutch Steam Packet Company (KPM) for the world exhibition in Paris which included a Balinese musical and dance group. Goris wrote captions for Spies' photographs describing the culture of the island for a broad audience. Westerners had an oddly ambivalent attitude about Bali. On the one hand they were vocal in the praises of the beauty of Bali and made them known to the world at large with texts and illustrations. On the other hand they attempted to protect the island against external influences. In the KPM publication to promote tourism Goris wrote: 'Regrettably, during the last few years tourists have been offered silver trinkets for sale, such as silver corks, powder boxes, bonbonniers etc. These, however have no real artistic value. Of course everyone should be free to purchase what they wish. But still, we believe we should advise against buying such articles, for two related reasons. First, there is the self-interest of the tourist who believes he is getting something truly Balinese and instead receives a mass-produced article with no real value. Second, there are the interests of Balinese craftsmen: in the face of the demand for such trinkets, silversmiths neglect their real handiwork, and the diminished production of real Balinese works of art makes it harder for tourists to acquire them.'

Ironically, Spies, who admired Balinese culture so much, had much influence on Balinese artists. For example, the young man Anak Agung Gede Soberat who came walking in curiously one day was advised by Spies to paint something other than traditional themes. Soberat and others following in his footsteps, such as Anak Agung Gede Meregeg, would become well-known Balinese painters.

Film

Greater than the effect of photographs was the effect of motion pictures. As early as 1926, Germans were filming on Bali; they filmed the famous and fantastical events of a temple festival, a cremation, and of course many forms of music and dance. The film directors were advised by Gregor Krause. This unconventional scholar had grown fond of the population and loved Balinese art. Although his ideas about the harmony of art and religion and his hostility towards the influence of Christianity were not always appreciated, his accurate descriptions of the most varied aspects of life on Bali were highly fascinating.

The films about Bali astounded viewers all over the world. Gradually Bali came to be seen as a paradise with bare-breasted smiling beauteous women, where the men danced themselves into a trance and the whole population lived from one festival to the next. The motion picture *Goona-Goona*, or The Kris, directed by the American André Roosevelt really managed to fling the myth of Bali out into the rest of the world. After seeing the film, people from all parts started dreaming of this faraway paradise, but only those who had the funds could afford to actually visit it. One of them was Noel Coward, who was quite taken aback by the bountiful Balinese culture. 'A civilized and pleasant person, with a sense of humour and zest for life', Spies wrote about him.

Another visitor to Bali, Charlie Chaplin, was disappointed that Bali was not the promiscuous island of his imagination. Coward wrote the following poem for Chaplin:

As I said this morning to Charlie
There is far too much music in Bali
And although as a place it's entrancing
There is also a thought too much dancing
It appears that each Balinese native
From the womb to the tomb is creative
And although the results are quite clever
There is too much artistic endeavour.

Left: SPIES, *Jungle scene with village*, undated, oil on canvas.

Vicky Baum's *Life and Death on Bali* was inspired by the island. 'Vicky is of course very enthusiastic, and like so many says she will return to stay a longer while', Spies wrote. Baum's novel was about the (fictional) discovery of a suitcase with diaries by the physician Fabius describing the *puputan* of 1908. Many people thought the character of Fabius was inspired by the German Dr. Krause. Baum ended the introduction to the novel with the complaint: 'Bali has become fashionable. When I returned from the island where in many places life and customs have remained unchanged for centuries, in the U.S. I encountered an invasion of Bali bars, Bali bathing suits and Bali songs. Needless to say, Dr. Fabius' book had nothing at all in common with that Bali — that Bali does not exist'.

The motion picture *Island of Demons*, made in 1930-31 by Victor Baron von Plessen with Spies' help, was also influential in shaping the image of Bali. Von Plessen was a German researcher, painter, author and motion picture maker who travelled throughout Asia, regularly lived amid isolated peoples and who reported his findings with articles, photographs and paintings. In 1924, when he was paying his first visit to the Indies, his attention was drawn to Walter Spies at the *kraton* of Jogyakarta. 'The Europeans stood in the great hall and talked about rubber prices', the baron remembered later. But Walter Spies stood to one side and was talking to aristocratic Javanese. Von Plessen passed on greetings from friends in Berlin and quickly made friends with Spies. Von Plessen turned out to be a Maecenas, stimulating Spies to make drawings of Bali, among other things. From time to time he would buy some of Spies' paintings. In February 1928 he traded his car for two canvases. 'It is a beautiful car', Spies wrote his mother. 'Very strong, and climbs the mountains like nothing else. I am learning to drive now'.

Time and again Von Plessen visited Spies and they would hold long conversations, drink whisky or watch dances. Von Plessen created the outline for the motion picture *Island of Demons* with the German scholar Dr. Dahlstein. Spies was the principal adviser. In the film, the tranquil life of a Balinese village is disturbed by the arrival of the witch Rangda. All sorts of dances and invocations are then employed to restore harmony. The makers of the film showed the peace and harmony of the island as well as the underlying current of magic, enchantment and invocation which is anchored in Balinese culture. One of the dances in the picture, the *kecak* dance from the *Ramayana*, was directed by Spies together with Rose Covarrubias; it is the spectacular monkey dance which is performed for tourists up to the present day.

Covarrubias

Rose Covarrubias was the wife of the painter and author Miguel Covarrubias, whose *Island of Bali* is still the standard work on Balinese culture. After husband and wife had gained some fame with a detailed and accurate work about Mexico, they went to Bali in 1930, after reading Gregor Krause's book about the island. After the usual reception at Buleleng and the tourist trip to Hotel Bali in Denpasar, Rose and Miguel quickly dropped the organized sightseeing programme to go out and discover the real Bali. They rented a house from a woodcarver and sought out Spies with a letter of introduction from the film director André Roosevelt. Spies was an unending source of information for their scientific work. 'The months flew past while we roamed around the island with Spies', Miguel Covarrubias wrote. 'We watched strange ceremonies, enjoyed the music, listened to fantastic tales, camped in the wild parts of western Bali or at the Sanur coral reef'. However, at times inspiration would drive Spies away from his friends and he would work on a painting in total isolation. The Covarrubiases made attempts to buy some of his canvases, but to no avail — Spies' paintings were sold before they were finished.

Margaret Mead

While Covarrubias described Bali as a paradise with an harmonious culture, an entirely different view was given some years later by the anthropologist Margaret Mead. Together with her husband, the versatile British scholar Bateson, she arrived in Bali in 1936. Margaret Mead did not let herself be deceived by appearances. Her research of many years conducted in the Pacific and on New Guinea and her remarkable reports and conclusions had elevated her to the status of a scholar who was to be taken seriously.

The Dutch colonial government was not entirely comfortable with the presence of the 'bohemians' on Bali: the western painters, writers and scholars whose lifestyles, in the eyes of the colonial administrators, were hardly worthy examples for the native population. Margaret Mead's request to marry Bateson (he would be her third husband) in Batavia was not granted. Many rumours had been started about her stay on New Guinea, where Mead had been living with her second husband, the New Zealander Reo Fortune, when Bateson arrived. After a tumultuous affair, Margaret Mead decided to leave her husband and to travel with Bateson. They were ultimately married on the ship that brought them to Bali. Margaret Mead met Spies through an introduction by the American scholar Jane Belo. At that time Spies was working with the anthropologist Beryl de Zoete on the book *Dance and Drama in Bali*.

Mead and Bateson were convinced that Balinese culture was so overorganized that the population lived under constant pressure and sought a way out through demonic dances, trance and emotional outbursts. They attempted to explain the behaviour of the Balinese in a Freudian manner as if that behaviour was mainly caused by frustration. Mead collected Balinese paintings which were to serve as evidence for her theories, and attempted to induce Balinese artists to depict their dreams and visions. She also employed photographs — thousands were taken, and many were published in her book *Balinese Character, A Photographic Analysis*, which appeared in 1942. The idea was that Balinese culture did not originate with India, China or Java but that it was wholly indigenous and influenced only in the course of time by Chinese and other cultures. The most important pictures for Mead's research were the photographs of gestures and facial expressions during dances, in trances or during emotional experiences.

Right: SPIES, *Road on Bali*, undated, oil on canvas.

Threat

Quite a few famous names found their way to Spies' door. It was often so crowded that he could hardly find the time to pursue his painting, music and other interests. It depressed him so much that in 1937 he had a cabin built in the mountains near Iseh, where he could escape when he wanted to work in peace. In the meantime the political situation changed quickly. The Dutch colonial administration was becoming more insecure, with the growing self-confidence of both the native population of the Indies as well as the small group of young Indonesians who were able to study in the Netherlands. On the one hand the Dutch attempted to create a politically conscious well-educated native elite, but on the other hand all resolute political activity was suppressed violently. Students in the Netherlands were kept under close supervision and sometimes their rooms were searched. Political activists in the Indies were exiled. In the meantime Europe suffered a major economic crisis, which proved to be fertile ground for the rise of National Socialism. Japan expanded into Asia and urged greater self-consciousness for native populations. The government in Batavia became increasingly nervous and compulsively it attempted to exemplify the western lifestyle. Dozens of Europeans who did not conform to moral standards were arrested, which caused a wave of fear, resulting in suicides, divorces and disappearances.

All this passed Walter Spies by; he received his guests, exalted Bali, and swam in the pool that he had built with the money the American movie star Barbara Hutton had paid for his paintings. Spies thought he was in favour with the Dutch colonial government: civil servants had often asked his advice about matters in remote desas, in 1935 he had been asked to organize a visit of the Governor General, and he had been consulted during the construction of a museum of Balinese art. On December 31, 1938 Spies wrote his mother a happy letter in which he told her about taking over two *gamelan* orchestras from Collin McPhee, a musicologist who had been working on Bali for years: 'I am very happy now because I posses two *gamelans*'. On the same day he was arrested by the Dutch authorities, accused of immoral behaviour and imprisoned until September 1939, in spite of the protests of Rudolf Bonnet and other friends.

Spies did not allow events to depress him. His letters remained cheerful. He translated Balinese fairytales in which he found inspiration for his paintings, and produced some of his best canvases. In a letter he laconically wrote that he painted so much because he finally had the peace he needed to work. At that time he also wrote to the German art dealer Neuhaus in Sanur, saying that music played an increasingly large part in his paintings. He compared the play of lines

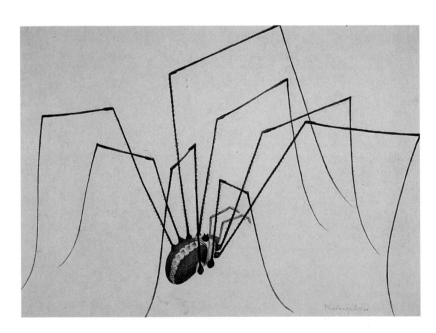

SPIES, *Spider*, undated, gouache and pencil.

64

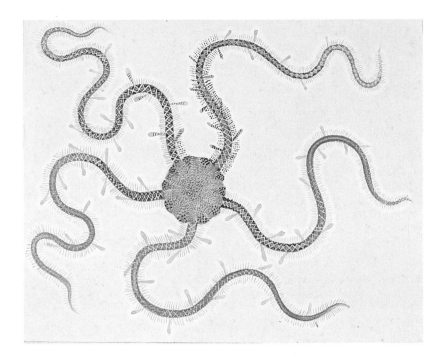

Right: SPIES, *Sea star*, undated, gouache and pencil.

and the contrasts between dark and light in his work to the themes and changing tempi in music. His letters shortly after his release were jubilant and relieved :'Life is one big birthday party', and he pitied the people 'who do not live life, who do not play it'.

Among those heartily welcoming Spies after his release was professor Baas Becking, director of the botanical gardens at Bogor. He brought Spies into contact with Dr. M.A. Lieftinck, director of the zoological museum, who encouraged him to observe insects and marine life. Lieftinck was full of praise for Spies: 'With inexhaustible energy and hunger for adventure, he sought out nature in the coral reefs, in forest streams and in the wild plants in his garden, diligently spending weeks doing his research. Soon, somewhere outdoors in a tent near the water, he was concentrating on painting colourful marine animals.' Spies became fascinated and painted a series of watercolours. He also started his own insect collection, often asking Lieftinck's advice: 'P.S. I have started collecting bees! But oh, oh, oh! Which are the wasps and which are the bees? For the time being I am catching anything I see and what does not clearly look like a wasp to me.'

Shortly thereafter the Second World War broke out. Germany invaded the Netherlands and immediately all Germans in the Netherlands East Indies were arrested, including Spies, the only remaining German on Bali. Spies had to leave his beloved island and ended up in a camp on Sumatra. Again, his optimism did not desert him, as it appears from his correspondence. In one of his last letters he is delighted to have received scores to the music of Rachmaninov: 'I am now busy writing out the voices of the orchestra — I still have some of the orchestration in my ears — and we will attempt to perform it here with our limited means. Rehearsing provides much satisfaction; I hope to be able to perform it for you. What a good time we are facing. I hope it will be possible to send you my last two paintings, but I have to wait a while because one has not dried yet. And it is uncertain whether the mail will continue to be regular. Again, thank you very, very much and all the best.'

Due to the Japanese threat to Sumatra, all Germans, including Spies, were put on board the ship *Van Imhoff* on January 18, 1942 for transport to Ceylon. A day later the ship was hit by a Japanese bomb and slowly started sinking. The Dutch crew abandoned ship, but the captain did not dare release the Germans without a clear order to do so. Spies, as well as most of the other internees, died horribly by drowning in the slowly sinking ship.

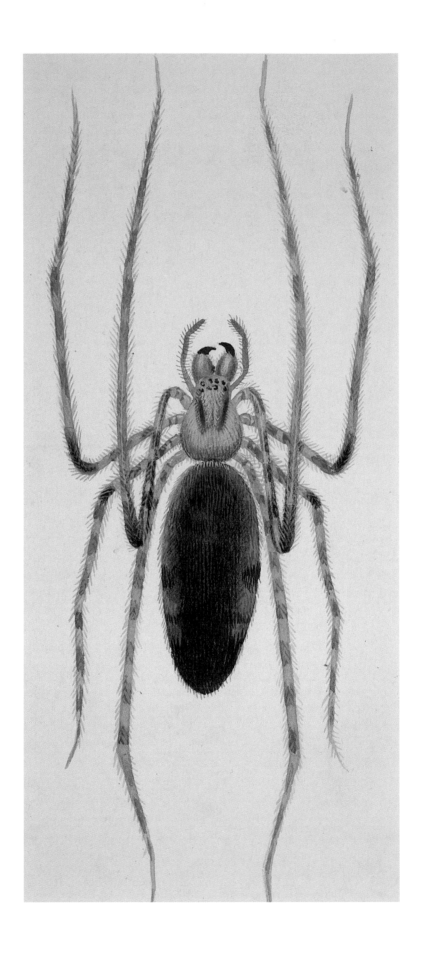

Left: SPIES, *Spider*, undated,
gouache and pencil.
Right: SPIES, *Dragonflies*, undated,
gouache and pencil.

Above: SPIES, *Balinese legend*,
undated, oil on canvas.
Right: SPIES, *Balinese legend*,
undated, oil on canvas.

Above: SPIES, *Landscape*, undated,
oil on canvas.
Left: SPIES, *Landscape*, undated,
oil on canvas.

NI - TJAWAN

BALI 1933

HOFKER

An Invitation

One day in February 1939, Walter Spies met Maria and Willem Hofker at his friend Bonnet's house. Spies was immediately interested in Maria's work, because she drew insects with great accuracy. Willem Hofker painted and made pastels, for which he preferred pretty Balinese girls as models. 'A Dutch couple has arrived, both of them painters, I met them a few days ago. They are truly nice friendly people, and I hope to see them often', Spies wrote to his mother. The couple had landed on Bali in 1938 under somewhat strange circumstances. The director of the Royal Dutch Steam Packet Company (KPM), J.E. Backer, had as much feeling for publicity as for talent. He understood that the increasing number of passengers who visited the Indonesian islands on his ships could be increased

Left: HOFKER, *Ni Tjawan*, 1938, oil on canvas.

even more by effective advertising. He asked the painter Willem Hofker to paint a portrait of Queen Wilhelmina for the KPM main office in Batavia, and to come present the portrait personally. Hofker was then given the opportunity to make paintings and drawings during a voyage with the KPM which were then to be reproduced for an advertising campaign. Although Hofker was not much of a traveller, he accepted the offer and left for the Indies after first thoroughly preparing himself with knowledge of the country and the language.

Models

Willem Hofker was born on May 3, 1902, into the family of a high-ranking civil servant in The Hague. His mother was an enthusiastic amateur writer and critic who closely followed the art and literature of the time. Young Willem soon proved to be a talented artist. Although his father's interest in art hardly extended to wishing an artistic career for his son, he finally gave in to pressure from a number of artists. Willem Hofker went to art school in The Hague and one year later to the Amsterdam Academy of Arts. He quickly developed into a talented draughtsman and etcher. When he graduated from the academy in 1924, he competed for the Prix de Rome and received second prize for a painting.

In 1928 he met Maria, the daughter of the painter Willem Rueter and two years later they were married. The couple settled in Amsterdam and in spite of the difficult thirties, when Europe was suffering a deep economic crisis, they were able to live off their art and to gain increasing recognition. Willem Hofker made paintings in warm colours or fine etches with subjects including still life, summer landscapes and town scenes. Hofker's strength was in his portraits; he was able to paint his models in relaxed realistic poses. Clothing and hair were painted with great skill, while the expression in the eyes on each of Hofker's portraits

draw attention because of their surprising naturalness. Soon Hofker became a portrait painter in great demand by Dutch society, and this finally led to the KPM commission mentioned earlier. The state portrait of Queen Wilhelmina was officially presented in 1938, in the KPM building on the Koningsplein in Batavia. It would stay there until the arrival of the Japanese, when it was publicly burned along with other symbols of the Dutch colonial administration.

On January 3, 1938 the Hofkers left for the Indies. On Java the Hofkers were struck by the beauty of the island. Willem tried to draw the populace, but time and again his models refused to be drawn due to the canon of Islam prohibiting visual depiction.

Travel was impeded when Hofker fell ill. They returned to Batavia and from there went to Bali. Through the mediation of the Dutch painter René Cockinga they found lodgings in a village on the South coast. Willem was soon impressed by the elegant

legong dancers and to his satisfaction he experienced that Balinese girls made no objection at all to freely posing. Hofker started a long series of oils and pastels of Balinese beauties in their dancing costumes, with sacrifices on their heads on their way to a temple, or busy with everyday chores.

The Hofkers soon felt at home on Bali and decided to stay. They found a house near Kerengang and lived a simple life amid the Balinese. On their searches for picturesque moments during temple ceremonies or dances by moonlight, the Hofkers met the American anthropologists Margaret Mead and Jane Belo, who were completely immersed in their scholarly work and

From left to right: HOFKER,
'Ni Njadat', 1939; *'Ni Rundit'*, 1939;
'Ni Wirea', 1943; *'Gusti Made
Toewi'*, 1943, pastel.

diligently made notes of everything they saw around them. The Hofkers kept in touch with the small group of western artists living on Bali, including Spies, Strasser, Meyer and of course their great friend Rudolf Bonnet. On the advice of the latter, they moved to Ubud in 1940.

The War

The outbreak of the Second World War brought an end to the idyllic life on Bali. The European artist community on Bali was suddenly divided into parties who were or were not involved in the conflict in Europe. Tourists had disappeared. The Australians and Americans hurried home; Germans had instantly become enemies and were arrested. The Dutch inhabitants were called up for military service. Hofker and Bonnet were required to report to the KNIL (Royal

Netherlands Indies Army) in Surabaya in December 1941, followed by a completely strange and unreal barracks life for both of them. Awkwardly and to the amusement of their fellow soldiers both men took part in exercises, gained attention for their marksmanship, but became popular, above all, through the drawings they made in their spare time. Hofker's drawings of Balinese girls were especially well-liked by the other soldiers.

The situation became more serious after the Japanese attack on Pearl Harbour. While Hofker and Bonnet were on leave on Bali, the Japanese landed at Sanur and the conditions became very dangerous. Initially, they hid in the caves of *Goa Gajah*, but quickly reached the conclusion that it was useless to hide on Bali. They came out of hiding and together with the other Europeans they were imprisoned in Denpasar.

In the beginning of the occupation, the Japanese attempted to win the sympathy of the native population by posing as their liberators from the former colonial rulers. The Dutch were belittled by, for example, forcing them to do small chores, a policy which was

not appreciated by many Balinese who did not wish to see this humiliation. The Japanese retained the native administration for practical purposes and attempted to promote the appreciation of Asian culture by, for example, organizing exhibitions of Balinese paintings and commissioning Balinese artists. The Balinese reaction was divided. Some expected a total revolution and new forms of democracy, while others were satisfied that the native administration originated by the Dutch was continued by the Japanese.

In prison, Bonnet was not able to find the peace and inspiration he needed to work, but Hofker made one drawing after the other. His occupations drew the attention of the Japanese commander, who promptly released Hofker and then after some negotiations also released his wife and his colleague Bonnet. The ostensible reason was that Japan did not imprison artists. Back in Ubud a time of limited freedom and great poverty followed, although the Balinese were always helpful. In December 1943 the relative freedom of the Dutch artists came to an end and the Hofkers and Bonnet were transported to prison camps on Celebes.

Prison Camps

The women were put in the prison camp Kampili; the men went to Pare-Pare. Willem Hofker had given his wife the paintings he had brought from Bali, hoping that with the women they would be safer from the Japanese. But when the women's camp was bombed near the end of the war, all those paintings and all of Maria's other possessions were destroyed. Life in Kampili and Pare-Pare was difficult, but compared to other Japanese prison camps in Indonesia they were an exception. Almost up to the end of the war there was always enough food, and the atrocities which were committed elsewhere did not occur in the camps on Celebes. The men did go through some difficult months when, after bombings by the Allies (who mistook the camps for Japanese bases), they were evacuated to a place high in the mountains where the cold nights caused much suffering. Willem Hofker had the strength and staying power to go on working, which of course was also a form of distraction from monotonous camp life. He drew his fellow prisoners in their deprived circumstances, depicted everyday activities such as sorting rice, sawing wood or working in the garden. These drawings later proved to be valuable as there was little other documentation of camp life.

The Japanese surrender was followed by a strange period. The Dutch government energetically attempted to reestablish the old colonial situation. But times had changed. The Indonesians were no longer willing to take up their old subservient roles. The released prisoners were for the time being unable to leave Celebes, yet Bonnet and Hofker vigorously worked to rebuilt their lives. They managed to save the teahouse the Japanese had started in the Grand Hotel in Makasar. Bonnet, who had made few drawings in the camp, burst loose in a wave of energy and painted the ceiling of the teahouse, and then created large murals in the

Left: HOFKER, *I Netis*, 1938, oil on canvas; *I Sangol*, 1939, pastel.
Above: HOFKER, *Bapak Degoen with his cock cages*, 1938, watercolour and pastel.

government house. A few months after the war an exhibition was organized in Makasar including works by Bonnet and Hofker.

Bonnet and Willem and Maria Hofker wished to return to Bali, but after a few months it was clear that the old days would never return. Hofker, like so many others, was called up for military service when the Dutch government decided to restore order by force. Bonnet was over fifty and thus exempt, and when finally in 1947 there was a ship for Bali, he returned to his beloved island. In the meantime Willem and Maria Hofker, unwilling to become embroiled in a war against their former friends, had left for the Netherlands. For years Willem Hofker was still making Balinese paintings and pastels after old sketches and notes but he would never see Bali again.

Above: HOFKER, *Ni Nyadet fetching water*, 1943; *Gusti Made Toewi*, 1943, pastel.
Right: HOFKER, *Ni Gusti Kompiang Mawar*, 1943, pastel.

Above: HOFKER, *Three women*,
1942, pastel.
Right: HOFKER, *Temple offerings*,
1938, pastel.

Bali – W.G. Hofker
1943

82

Left: HOFKER, *Gusti Nyoman
Klepon*, 1943, pastel.
Above: HOFKER, *Balinese girl in
three poses*, 1943, pastel.

Above: HOFKER, *Balinese girl
dressed as Galut*, 1938, pastel.
Right: HOFKER, *Ni Tjawan*, 1938,
pastel and gouache.

Left: HOFKER, *Anak Agoeng
Ngoerah*, 1941, pastel and gouache.
Above: HOFKER, *Village scene in
Sanur*, undated, oil on canvas.

HOFKER: *Offerings for Jero Gede*,
1940, oil on canvas.

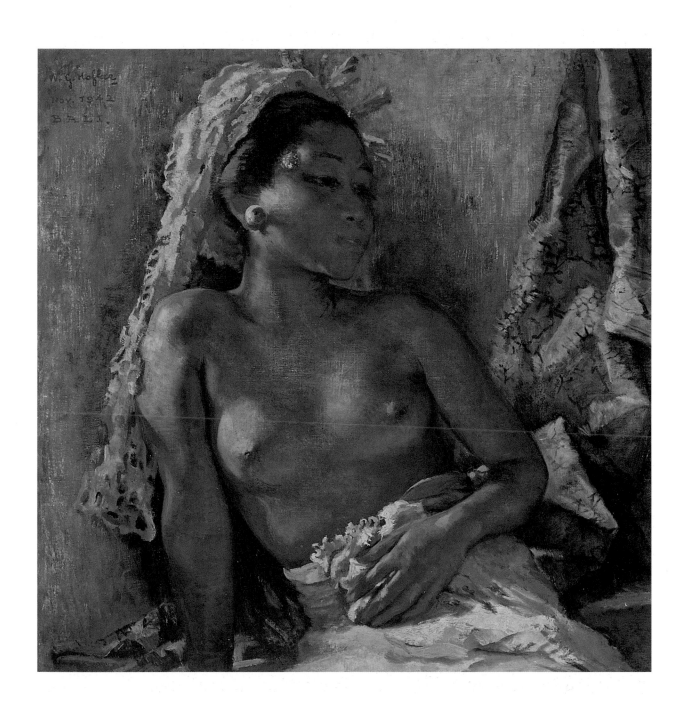

HOFKER: *Ni Kenyung*, 1942, oil on
canvas.

Left: HOFKER, *Ni Noneh*, 1941,
pastel.
Below: HOFKER, *Girl at temple*,
undated, pastel.
Below right: HOFKER, *Girl at the
Campuan Temple*, 1943, pastel and
gouache.

Above left: HOFKER, *Campuan Temple in Ubud*, 1943, pastel.
Above: HOFKER, *Temple in Kesiman*, 1940, pastel.
Right: HOFKER, *Temple in Pagan, Denpasar*, 1938, pastel.

Tempel in Pagan, — Denpasar

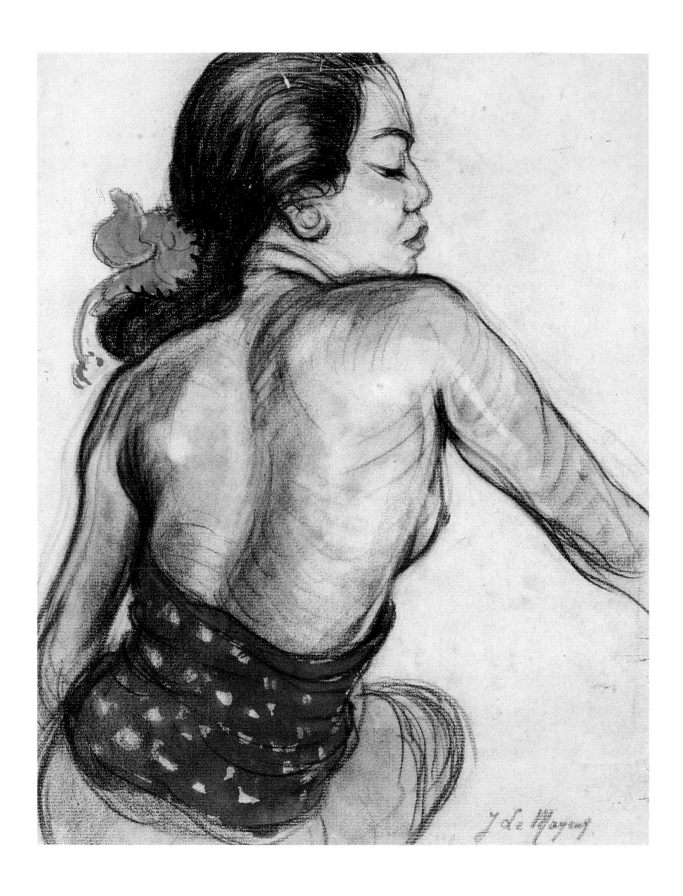

LE MAYEUR

In his native Belgium the artist Adrien Jean Le Mayeur de Merpres found little recognition for his work and his patrician family saw him as a freebooting adventurer. Unsurprisingly therefore, the artist decided to leave Europe behind and seek his fortune in the exotic Orient. In 1932, at the age of 52, he arrived on Bali. He would remain there until shortly before his death. In his lodgings in the South of Bali he feverishly worked at an exhibition which was to be held in Singapore. From the beginning he was fascinated by temple rituals and dances. He was also impressed by the girl Ni Pollok whom he met on an occasion when she was dancing the *legong*. At the exhibition in Singapore in the beginning of 1933 more than thirty pastels and paintings of Le Mayeur's were shown; all of them had to do with Bali and had titles like *Rosy Morning, Balinese Dancer, Beach Impressions*, and

Balinese Weaver. The press was enthusiastic about the exhibition. One paper wrote: 'The artist has produced coloured pictures without entering into great detail', which was an accurate description of Le Mayeur's airy post-impressionism. Almost all his work was sold and the painter decided to return to the island that attracted and inspired him. He bought a piece of land at the beach of Sanur and built a house there and laid out a beautiful garden.

Ni Pollok

In the meantime Ni Pollok had reached the age of sixteen, which was too old according to Balinese tradition to dance the *legong*. She now had enough time to pose for Le Mayeur and very soon became his lover and only model. From that time onwards Ni Pollok figured in a wide variety of ways on dozens of paintings. In 1935 the painter married the girl who was then eighteen. In contrast to other European painters like

Left: LE MAYEUR, *Ni Pollok*, undated, crayon and gouache.

Bonnet, Spies and Hofker, Le Mayeur was not interested in Balinese painters and their art. There was little contact between them and Le Mayeur. From an extensive survey that Margaret Mead made among dozens of painters from Batuan and Sanur it appears that only two of the Balinese artists had ever seen the painter and some of his work.

In 1941 Le Mayeur had another exhibition in Singapore. Besides work he had done on Bali he presented work he had done earlier with scenes from Belgium, India and Venice. Ni Pollok could be seen in elegant dancing poses. Shortly afterwards the war broke out. The Japanese did not intern Le Mayeur because of his Belgian nationality, but he was put under house arrest. When, as a result of the war, painting materials were no longer available, Le Mayeur used rough jute for canvas. He often used crayon and very probably also natural paints like those traditionally used by the Balinese. Although Le Mayeur came through the war without many problems, he certainly did not have pleasant memories of the years in which tourism had totally disappeared and so many of his colleagues and friends had fled or were imprisoned in camps.

Museum

After the war, tourism slowly made a comeback. The myth of Bali gained new life with songs as in Rogers' and Hammerstein's 1949 musical *South Pacific*, in which the choir brightly sings: 'Come to me, come to me; Here am I, your special island; If you try, you'll find me; Where the sky meets the sea; Here am I your special island; Come to me, come to me; Balihai, Balihai, Balihai.'

In voyages organized by the KPM, visits to the artist in Sanur were included as an extra attraction. Le Mayeur usually walked around bare-chested and in beige bermudas. Ni Pollok patiently posed for the lenses of thousands of cameras and produced the most delicious meals. The couple's hospitality was boundless. In the March 1951 issue of National Geographic Magazine it was even reported: 'Though people wander in and out their house all day, Le Mayeur's hospitality is unending'. Tourists eagerly bought paintings from the Belgian Balinese, and in that way his work became part of many collections all over the world.

In those years Le Mayeur's health was often less than good. He regularly suffered from malaria, which

increasingly weakened him. In 1948 he fell off his little horse Gipsy and broke a leg. The painter, now 68 years old, never entirely recovered and from then on needed a cane. In 1951 the old artist was assaulted by a group of robbers and it was only with great difficulty and with assistance called in by Ni Pollok that the criminals were driven off. The painter had received a large stab wound in the shoulder.

After the uneasy fifties, peace returned to daily life on Bali and the stream of tourists greatly increased. Sukarno, much charmed by Ni Pollok, bought two large canvases for his art collection. Although the old painter's work exhibited less strong brush strokes compared to his earlier work and the figures appeared to be less coherent, he remained a colourist *pur sang*, with a palette on which the colour green was increasingly important.

In 1958 Le Mayeur travelled to Brussels with his wife for treatment of cancer of the ear. The illness proved terminal and the painter died on May 31, 1958. Ni Pollok returned to Bali and married an Italian physician who, like so many foreigners in those troubled times, had his residence permit revoked and was obliged to leave. Ni Pollok stayed behind on Bali. As Le

Mayeur had provided in his will, she was allowed to live in the house in Sanur up to her death in 1985. The house and its contents, including a hundred paintings by Le Mayeur, were then donated to the Indonesian government and converted into a museum.

From left to right: LE MAYEUR, *Two women inside a house*, undated; *Women dancing*, undated; *Two women weaving*, undated; *Three women*, undated, oil on canvas.

Left: LE MAYEUR, *Ni Pollok with fan*, undated, crayon and water-colour.

Below: LE MAYEUR, *Girl in a palm plantation*, undated, crayon and watercolour.

Right: LE MAYEUR, *Women dancing*, undated, oil on canvas.

Above: LE MAYEUR, *Two women weaving*, undated, oil on canvas.
Left above: LE MAYEUR, *Three women in a garden*, undated, oil on canvas.
Left: LE MAYEUR, *Three women arranging flowers*, undated, oil on canvas.

LE MAYEUR, *Five women at a lotus
pond*, undated, oil on canvas.

LE MAYEUR, *Bathing in the garden*,
undated, oil on canvas.

Pages 104-105: LE MAYEUR, *Four girls at a lotus pond*, undated, oil on canvas.

Above: LE MAYEUR, *Two women with parasol*, undated, oil on canvas.

Right: LE MAYEUR, *On the beach*, undated, oil on canvas.

SMIT

Bali in the Fifties

'I wrote my father that here on Bali it is like the seventeenth century. You can't imagine that now. There was no traffic in the streets. Electricity did not arrive until 1968 when the Bali Beach Hotel was built. I have lived with a paraffin lamp for twenty-five years. We had bamboo lamps with paper sides. Those gave beautiful light. Bonnet loved them. Sometimes he would decorate his whole garden with them. Outside you only heard the barking of dogs. During their mating times you could hear their howling, a sound as from the Middle Ages. The houses were made of clay, like the walls around the yards. When you approached a village you walked under an archway of dark *Waringin* trees. When you came out you would be in full sunlight again, with sawahs everywhere, laid out in terraces. Bali has been made by the Balinese. The *sawahs*, houses, temples, decorations, everything. Life in the fifties was simple and cheap. For a *kepeng*, about a quarter cent, you could buy fruit in the market. For a U.S. dollar you could buy a large painting.'

In his house on Bali, next to the Neka Museum which was extended to include an Arie Smit Pavilion in December 1994, Arie Smit recounts the Bali of the fifties. On the hills of Sanggingan a cool breeze is blowing. Down by the river, which at the end of the dry season has reached its lowest level, there is the monotonous sound of a stonemason. Flying lizards glide from one palm tree to the other, and crawl up the trunks looking for insects. In 1956 Arie Smit settled on Bali for good. It was a strange time, after the terrors of the so-called Police Actions which ended with the long overdue Dutch recognition of the Indonesian Republic. The founding of the young state, in 1945, was accompanied by conflicts between the various parties, lack of understanding between older and younger generations, and great social change.

Left: SMIT, *Orchids*, 1991,
oil on canvas.

SMIT, *Village of Ubud*, 1971,
oil on canvas.

These changes also affected Bali, and artists like I Negendon and Ida Bagus Made contributed to raising the level of consciousness of artists and scholars. Anak Agung, attentive to the altered balance of power, played an important part in national politics. In the meantime, art on Bali was back at the level it had reached in the thirties. There were hardly any tourists. Bonnet did his best to inspire the artists to work on in the tradition of the *Pita Maha* until he was obliged to leave Indonesia. Arie Smit had his own unique place. In spite of his modesty and reticence, after the Second World War he became the most important stimulator of painting on Bali.

Topographical Service

Arie Smit was born on April 15, 1916 in the town of Zaandam, in an environment typical of foreign stereotypes of Holland: lush green meadows, much water, windmills and wooden shoes. But Arie Smit was already fantasizing about the tropics at an early age, due to the tales of an Indonesian school friend. His chance came in 1938 when he was drafted into the Army and was sent out to the Netherlands East Indies. He was stationed with the topographical service, where he acquired his graphic technique. He drew, illustrated books, occupied himself with design and was very interested in the work of the artists depicting Indonesia which was regularly exhibited in Batavia. While working on contour maps of Bali, he planned to visit the island. But it would take years before Smit would really accomplish that. The war broke out and Arie Smit was sent to prison camps in Thailand and Burma, where he suffered through one of the worst types of forced labour of the war: building railroads through the jungle.

After the war he returned to his old job at the topographical service. As the political situation became more tense, more Dutch left Indonesia. Smit remained, and when Indonesian independence was recognized by the Netherlands in December 1949, he was one of the few to become an Indonesian citizen, which was a great step in those uncertain times. He taught graphic technique at the Bandung Technical Institute and exhibited in Jakarta, Bandung, Palembang and other Indonesian cities. Both his work and his conscious choice for Indonesia was appreciated by many Indonesians. In 1956 Smit settled on Bali, where two other Dutch artists were working: Rudolf Bonnet, who had retained his Dutch nationality, and the painter Hans Snel, who, like Smit, had come to Indonesia as a soldier, albeit not until after the Second World War. Arie Smit first lived in Ubud where he met the connoisseur and art dealer James Clarence Pandy, who helped him get a studio in Sanur and who exhibited his work.

The 'Young Artists'

Smit would become responsible for the development of a new shoot on the trunk of Balinese art. The inspiration occurred during a walk on a day in 1960 in the neighbourhood of Penestanan. Two young tenders of ducks were killing time by drawing pictures in the sand; Arie Smit was struck by the originality of the drawings and offered to teach them to work with paint. The boys' parents at first objected, but when substitute labour had been arranged, I Nyoman Cakra and I Ketut Soki were given the opportunity to follow art lessons. Smit taught them painting techniques, but let them choose their own subjects and colours. During the lessons he circumspectly put his own paintings out of sight, knowing that on Bali the highest compliment of a student to a teacher was copying the latter's work. Smit did not need to help the boys choose a subject. 'Balinese education is visual', Smit explains. 'Look and look again and then try it yourself. No shortage of stories. Hinduism is one big narrative'.

The result of Smit's lessons were surprising works with clear colours and strong contours. It was soon appreciated and was quickly bought by collectors and tourists who came to Bali in increasing numbers during the sixties. Smit acquired more and more students.

Parents who thought their sons could draw, came to see Arie Smit with a fried chicken and asked him to teach their children. If there was sufficient talent, Smit would agree. Soon dozens of boys were being taught by Smit, always in the same reserved way. A 'school' came into existence, which became known as the 'Young Artists'; its followers mostly came from Penestanan. In 1970 the 'Young Artists' exhibited outside Bali for the first time, at an exhibition in the Singapore National Museum .

Below left: SMIT, *Tropical landscape*, 1974, oil on canvas.
Below: SMIT, *Shrines beneath the Banyan*, 1972, oil on canvas.

The Mood of Bali

In the meantime Arie Smit was very active. He roamed about in Bali, moved house 36 times, made sketches everywhere and expounded upon them in his paintings of temples, flowers, sea views and rice fields, bathed in the light of the moon or caressed by the setting sun. His work is characterized by strong lines and an expressionist tone. Arie Smit seldom paints real landscapes or accurately represented temples in realistic colours. He expresses an idea in lines and textures, and with his warm colours he conjures up the mood of Bali. But besides these detailed canvases of temples and landscapes he also paints figures, such as the beautiful lithograph of the squatting *Boy in Blue.*

In 1967 Smit met Suteja Neka, a driven art dealer and collector who was able to make a dream come true in 1976 with the founding of the Neka Museum, which, by means of a tastefully compiled collection, has been able to provide a clear overview of Balinese art and art created on Bali by foreign artists. The contacts between

Above: SMIT, *Village in Bali,* 1973, oil on canvas.
Right: SMIT, *Rice field panorama,* 1973, oil on canvas

Smit and Neka led to a fruitful cooperation, which enabled Smit to concentrate on his work and build up a large oeuvre. Arie Smit's work is appreciated by many and forms part of collections in Indonesia and all over the world, but oddly enough is scarcely found in the Netherlands. The artist's labours were rewarded by exhibitions and important citations, but Smit remains imperturbable and with unflagging interest he continues to follow the developments of art on his beloved island.

SMIT, *Temple gate*, 1973,
oil on canvas.

SMIT, *Temple gate*, 1979,
oil on canvas.

Above: SMIT, *Balinese youth*,
1980, acrylic on canvas.
Left: SMIT, *Portrait of a Balinese
youth*, 1988, acrylic on canvas.
Right: SMIT, *Resting*, 1981,
oil on canvas.

Left: SMIT, *Boy in the garden*, 1990, oil on canvas.
Below: SMIT, *Banyan tree*, 1990, oil on canvas.
Right: SMIT, *Dreaming of his village*, 1986, oil on canvas.

Left above: SMIT, *Landscape with temple*, 1984, oil on canvas.
Left below: SMIT, *Sawah landscape*, 1991, oil on canvas.
Right: SMIT, *Gnarled Banyan tree*, 1992, acrylic on paper.
Below: SMIT, *Young man in a contemplative mood*, 1992, oil on canvas.

SMIT, *Landscape*, 1993,
oil on canvas.

SMIT, *High tide*, 1993,
acrylic on canvas.

SMIT, *Village in Klungkung*, 1994,
oil on canvas.

SMIT, *Corner of the village*, 1993,
acrylic on canvas.

SMIT, *Full moon ceremony*, 1994,
oil on canvas.

SMIT, *Coral temple in Sanur*, 1994,
acrylic on canvas.

Acknowledgements

The publishers are greatly indebted to Arend de Roever and Mr Suteja Neka. Special thanks are due to Drs. J. Ubbens for his textual assistance for the chapter on Le Mayeur.

All works by Nieuwenkamp were photographed by Cary Venselaar, and are from the collection of the Stichting Nieuwenkamp, c/o Mr J.F.K. Kits Nieuwenkamp, 3451 ST Vleuten, The Netherlands.
Photography at the Neka Museum was carried out by Koes Karnadi, and at Sandalwood BV and the majority of private collections by Wouter Thorn-Leeson.

Illustration credits and sizes of the original works

front cover, Sandalwood BV, 30 x 30 cm
back cover, Neka Museum, Bali, 36 x 45 cm
p. 5, private collection, 115 x 82 cm
p. 6, Neka Museum, Bali, 93 x 96 cm
p. 8, courtesy Christie's, 74 x 46 cm
p. 11, Neka Museum, Bali, 31 x 57 cm
p. 12, Stichting Museum Nieuwenkamp
p. 14, Stichting Museum Nieuwenkamp
p. 16, Stichting Museum Nieuwenkamp
p. 17, Stichting Museum Nieuwenkamp
p. 19, Stichting Museum Nieuwenkamp
p. 20, Stichting Museum Nieuwenkamp
p. 21, Stichting Museum Nieuwenkamp
p. 22, Stichting Museum Nieuwenkamp
p. 23, Stichting Museum Nieuwenkamp
p. 24, Stichting Museum Nieuwenkamp
p. 25, Stichting Museum Nieuwenkamp
p. 26, Stichting Museum Nieuwenkamp
p. 27, Stichting Museum Nieuwenkamp
p. 28, Stichting Museum Nieuwenkamp
p. 29, Stichting Museum Nieuwenkamp
p. 30, Stichting Museum Nieuwenkamp
p. 31, Stichting Museum Nieuwenkamp
p. 32, Stichting Museum Nieuwenkamp
p. 33, Stichting Museum Nieuwenkamp
p. 34, Stichting Museum Nieuwenkamp
p. 35, Stichting Museum Nieuwenkamp
p. 36, Sandalwood BV, 62 x 43 cm
p. 38 top, below left and middle, private collection
p. 38 below right, Sandalwood BV, 55 x 42 cm
p. 41 left, Sandalwood BV, 35 x 29 cm
p. 41 right, Sandalwood BV, 64 x 45 cm
p. 42, Sandalwood BV, 47 x 37 cm
p. 43 left, Sandalwood BV, 23 x 20 cm
p. 43 right, Sandalwood BV, 43 x 36 cm
p. 44, courtesy Sotheby's, 115 x 79 cm
p. 45, private collection
p. 46, private collection
p. 47, courtesy Sotheby's, 66 x 84 cm
p. 48, Sandalwood BV, 31 x 25 cm
p. 49, Sandalwood BV, 46 x 37 cm
p. 50 top, Yu-Chee Chong Fine Art, London, 40 x 56 cm
p. 50 below left, Sandalwood BV, 40 x 36 cm
p. 50 below right, Sandalwood BV, 40 x 34 cm
p. 51, private collection
p. 52, private collection
p. 53, Sandalwood BV, 60 x 86 cm
p. 54, courtesy KIT, Amsterdam, 101 x 83 cm
p. 57, courtesy KIT, Amsterdam, 105 x 90 cm
p. 58, courtesy KIT, Amsterdam, 45 x 80 cm
p. 60, courtesy Gleerum, 92 x 70 cm
p. 63, courtesy KIT, Amsterdam, 75 x 45 cm
p. 64, Natural History Museum, Leyden
p. 65, Sandalwood BV, 24 x 30 cm
p. 66, Natural History Museum, Leyden

p. 67 top, Natural History Museum, Leyden, 13 x 18 cm
p. 67 middle, Natural History Museum, Leyden, 16 x 23 cm
p. 67 bottom, Natural History Museum, Leyden, 18 x 23 cm
p. 68, courtesy KIT, Amsterdam, 81 x 66 cm
p. 69, private collection, 80 x 65 cm
p. 70, courtesy Gleerum, 92 x 70 cm
p. 71, courtesy Christie's, 62 x 91 cm
p. 72, courtesy Gleerum, 86 x 62 cm
p. 74 left, courtesy Christie's, 40 x 30 cm
p. 74 right, Neka Museum, Bali, 48 x 30 cm
p. 75 left, courtesy Christie's, 31 x 23 cm
p. 75 right, Neka Museum, Bali, 51 x 27 cm
p. 76 left, courtesy Gleerum, 39 x 28 cm
p. 76 right, courtesy Gleerum, 32 x 25 cm
p. 77, courtesy Christie's, 35 x 21 cm
p. 78 left, Neka Museum, Bali, 46 x 30 cm
p. 78 right, Neka Museum, Bali, 52 x 35 cm
p. 79, Neka Museum, Bali, 36 x 47 cm
p. 80, Neka Museum, Bali, 32 x 23 cm
p. 81, Neka Museum, Bali, 45 x 32 cm
p. 82, Neka Museum, Bali, 47 x 29 cm
p. 83, Neka Museum, Bali, 46 x 30 cm
p. 84, courtesy Sotheby's, 46 x 31 cm
p. 85, private collection, 50 x 28 cm
p. 86, courtesy Gleerum, 45 x 28 cm
p. 87, courtesy Gleerum, 44 x 52 cm
p. 88, Neka Museum, Bali, 30 x 30 cm
p. 89, Neka Museum, Bali, 53 x 52 cm
p. 90, Neka Museum, Bali, 47 x 30 cm
p. 91 left, courtesy Christie's
p. 91 right, Neka museum, Bali, 47 x 30 cm
p. 92 left, Neka Museum, Bali, 53 x 35 cm
p. 92 right, Neka Museum, Bali, 35 x 32 cm
p. 93, Neka museum, Bali, 52 x 36 cm
p. 94, courtesy Christie's, 36 x 26 cm
p. 96 left, courtesy Christie's, 78 x 91 cm
p. 96 right, courtesy Christie's, 75 x 90 cm
p. 97 left, courtesy Christie's, 78 x 91 cm
p. 97 right, courtesy Christie's, 78 x 91 cm
p. 98 top, private collection, c. 21 x 30 cm
p. 98 bottom, Sandalwood BV
p. 99, Yu-Chee Chong Fine Art, London
p. 100 top, courtesy Gleerum, 100 x 120 cm
p. 100 bottom, courtesy Gleerum, 55 x 65 cm
p. 101, Sandalwood BV, 75 x 90 cm
p. 102, courtesy Gleerum, 100 x 120 cm
p. 103, courtesy Gleerum, 97 x 119 cm
p. 104, Yu-Chee Chong Fine Art, London
p. 106, private collection, 53 x 63 cm
p. 107, courtesy Christie's, 46 x 56 cm
p. 108, Neka Museum, Bali, 92 x 92 cm
p. 110, Sandalwood BV, 59 x 47 cm
p. 111 left, Neka Museum, Bali, 70 x 48 cm
p. 111 right, Neka Museum, Bali, 58 x 45 cm
p. 112, Neka Museum, Bali, 52 x 65 cm
p. 113, Neka Museum, Bali, 52 x 64 cm
p. 114, courtesy Christie's, 52 x 52 cm
p. 115, Neka Museum, Bali, 54 x 50 cm
p. 116 top, Neka Museum, Bali, 75 x 75 cm
p. 116 bottom, Neka Museum, Bali, 75 x 75 cm
p. 117, Neka Museum, Bali, 80 x 80 cm
p. 118 top, Neka Museum, Bali, 50 x 60cm
p. 118 bottom, Neka Museum, Bali, 48 x 72 cm
p. 119, Neka Museum, Bali, 65 x 50 cm
p. 120 top, courtesy Christie's, 31 x 39 cm
p. 120 bottom, courtesy Christie's, 30 x 34 cm
p. 121 top, Neka Museum, Bali, 57 x 42 cm
p. 121 bottom, Neka Museum, Bali, 46 x 48 cm
p. 122, Neka Museum, Bali, 70 x 93 cm
p. 123, Neka Museum, Bali, 145 x 145 cm
p. 124, Neka Museum, Bali, 73 x 96 cm
p. 125, Neka Museum, Bali, 145 x 145 cm
p. 126, Neka Museum, Bali, 71 x 96 cm
p. 127, Neka Museum, Bali, 149 x 144 cm